Polar Bear, Arctic Hare

Poems of the Frozen North

EILEEN SPINELLI

ILLUSTRATIONS BY

EUGENIE FERNANDES

WORDSONG

AN IMPRINT OF HIGHLIGHTS

Honesdale, Pennsylvania

To the DeMott family
—ES

For Owen
—EF

The publisher thanks Dr. David R. Klein, emeritus professor of wildlife ecology, Institute of Arctic Biology and Department of Biology and Wildlife, University of Alaska, Fairbanks, for reviewing the text and illustrations of this book.

WordSong
An Imprint of Highlights
815 Church Street
Honesdale, Pennsylvania 18431
Printed in China

Library of Congress Cataloging-in-Publication Data

Spinelli, Eileen.
Polar bear, arctic hare : poems of the frozen North / Eileen Spinelli ; Illustrations by Eugenie Fernandes.
p. cm.
ISBN: 978-1-59078-344-3 (hc) • 978-1-62979-112-8 (pb)
1. Animals—Arctic regions—Juvenile poetry. 2. Arctic Regions—Juvenile poetry. 3. Children's poetry,
American. I. Fernandes, Eugenie, ill. II. Title.
PS3569.P5457P65 2006
811'.54—dc22
2006012623

First paperback edition, 2014
Book design by Lucas Weidner
The text of this book is set in Sabon.
The illustrations are done in acrylic.

10 9 8 7 6 5 4 3 2 1

POLAR BEAR,
ARCTIC HARE

TABLE OF CONTENTS

POLAR BEAR FAMILY

Polar bear mama moves with grace
to find a sheltered winter place.
She digs a snow cave wide and deep
where she and baby cubs can sleep.

Come spring, the cubs set out for fun.
They romp all day in the Arctic sun.
They slip and slide. They race and roam.
Then, weary, ride their mama home.

6

GENTLE ORANGE-GOLDEN BUMBLEBEE

The Arctic bumblebee can sting
if it so has a mind to—
although it's rather nice to know
it seldom seems inclined to.

SNOWBIRDS

Are those giant snowflakes?
No!
Those are buntings
flying low,
seeking seeds in melting snow.
O so pretty buntings.

CHAMPION TRAVELER

Arctic tern,
Wings unfurled,
Flies halfway
Around the world.

From the South Pole
To the North—
Chasing summer,
Back and forth.

Fast birds, slow birds,
Big birds, small—
Arctic tern
Outflies them all.

9

ARCTIC SUN

In early June the Arctic sun
illuminates the day.
It spangles melting ice
and lingering snow.
It sparkles on the wings
of glaucous gull
who's come to nest
and watch her babies grow.

In early June the Arctic sun
holds to the sky
and plays the part of moon
throughout the night.
It shimmers on the dreams
of Arctic hare
and splashes sleepy weasel
with its light.

10

Arctic Poppy

Arctic poppy,
fragile, gold,
seeds itself
in Arctic cold.
Gleams in sunlight,
scents the breeze,
beckons butterflies
and bees.
Blooms—but not
for very long.
Short and sweet
the poppy's song.

11

ARCTIC NURSERY RHYME

Arctic tundra,
Arctic tundra,
How does your garden grow?
With lupine seeds
And fireweeds
And bearberries all in a row.

12

RACING THE PEREGRINE FALCON

Faster than a school bus.
Faster than a hare.
Faster than a racecar.
Faster than a bear.
Faster than a cheetah—
The awesome peregrine.
I think I'll save my running shoes
For races I can win!

CARIBOU

Across the tundra
Caribou coming.
Racing and chasing
Caribou coming.
Thrumming and drumming
Caribou coming.
Romping and stomping
Caribou coming.
Hammering, clamoring
Caribou coming.
Thundering, rumbling
Caribou coming.
In waves, cascades
Caribou coming
  and coming
    and coming
      and coming
        and coming.

SAFE AND WARM

Arctic winter finds the lemming
tunneling under snow unseen—
deep away from prowling owl—
until the willow leaves turn green.

15

BELUGA

Beluga.
Trapped beneath the ice
rams his head against it—twice.
The ice gives way. Beluga crashes
upward as the dark sea splashes.
He takes a mighty gulp of air.
He bumps a startled polar bear.
He interrupts some seals at play.
Then, satisfied, he swims away.
Beluga.

RUDE AWAKENING

If you should awaken
Arctic walrus,
be prepared
for quite a flap.
Usually a peaceful fellow,
nothing makes him
fuss or bellow
like an interrupted nap.

17

MUSK-OX

Looks a lot like buffalo
Standing silent in the snow.

Yet that shaggy woolly coat
Makes him more akin to goat.

18

PTARMIGAN

Most other birds
Who soar with summery grace
Depart when Arctic winter
Shows its face.
Not the ptarmigan.

She stays,
With feathery snowshoes
On her feet
And sometimes only
Buds from twigs to eat.
Hardy ptarmigan.

Then finding space
Behind a heap of rocks,
She sleeps and hides
From hungry Arctic fox.
O ever clever ptarmigan.

19

SHADOW

On silent wings
the snowy owl takes flight—
a scrap of fog
across the Arctic night.

CHOIR LOBO

Wolf howls,
gathering the scattered pack.
Parents, offspring
race across a treeless track.
Aunts and uncles
join the group to croon,
starkly silhouetted by
a silvered Arctic moon.

21

GUESS

What's black and white
(but not a penguin)?
What's fast and fierce
(but not a bear)?
What lives in pods
(but not a pea)?
What swims the deep
(but breathes the air)?
What eats a lot
(but not a hog)?
What leaps to life
(but not a quail)?
What has sharp teeth
(but not a shark)?
Answer, please:
The killer whale.

ICEBERG

Castle of ice
Rising from the sea.
Jagged spires,
Lonely walls
Stand against
The swirling squalls
Shimmering silently.

HUMP OF SNOW

Hump of snow . . .
Hopping?
No!
Snow can't hop
Or thump
Or stare.
Hump of snow
Is
Arctic hare.

Snow Flea

Tiny, wingless snow flea freezes
overnight as stiff as tin.
Does he mind or even notice
just what sort of state he's in?
Things warm up and—leaping lizards!—
snow flea's jumping as before,
none the worse for being frozen
on the icy Arctic shore.

OCEAN ICE

Bobbing
Shifting
Clicking
Clacking
Groaning
Drifting
Rolling
Cracking
Roaring
Thrusting
In the air
Heaving
Crushing
Boats beware!

NARWHAL SIGHTING

What *is* that in the Arctic sea?
That creature with a single horn?
Some sailors saw it long ago
And thought it was a unicorn.

27

WARNING

Ringed seal
half dozing
on the ice,
believing this
is paradise—
the mellow sun,
the summer air—
are you aware
that polar bear
is sliding down
that bank of snow?
Ringed seal,
I think
you'd better
go!

LISTEN

Seals slurp.
Buntings trill.
Whales chirp.
Ravens shrill.
Wolves howl.
Walrus roar.
Bears growl.
Lemmings snore.
Listen, child,
Owls whooooooooo.
Perhaps the wild
Is calling you!

ARCTIC FACTS

The ARCTIC HARE is the largest of all hares. Some are surprisingly tame. When startled, the Arctic hare usually runs uphill.

One of the largest members of the dog family, the ARCTIC WOLF is an ardent, fearless hunter. It fluffs up its fur to give its coat warm air pockets. You may also call it the tundra wolf or the white wolf.

Blue-flowered ARCTIC LUPINE grows to two feet tall. It can cover meadows of many acres.

BEARBERRIES come in two colors: red and black. Many Arctic animals eat this fruit. Its wrinkled leaves turn bright red in the fall.

In order to make seeds, the ARCTIC POPPY needs as much warmth as possible. So as the sun moves across the sky, the poppy turns slowly to face it. Some Arctic poppies are yellow. Some are white.

There is only one white whale—the BELUGA. Because of the beluga's whistling, chirping sounds, sailors used to call it the sea canary.

The ARCTIC TERN is the long-distance champion of the world. Every year it flies from the Arctic to the Antarctic and back again, following the summer sun—a round trip of more than twenty-two thousand miles!

CARIBOU are similar to reindeer. Vast herds roam Arctic pastures. The hooves of the caribou spread out to form a kind of snowshoe, good for walking on the snow and for digging through it to find winter food.

LEMMINGS live in tunnels beneath the snow. It is the blanket of snow, along with their coat of heavy fur, that keeps them warm. They look like chubby mice.

This animal has two names. In winter, with its fur coat of white, it's the ERMINE. In summer, the coat turns brown, and ermine's name changes to WEASEL. The ermine-weasel is curious and playful.

The long shaggy coat of the MUSK-OX keeps it warm in the worst blizzards. When threatened by predators, these animals form a circle for protection, with the youngsters in the middle.

FIREWEED's spikes of purple-pink flowers brighten the brief Arctic summer. Fireweed is also known as willow herb. The dwarf fireweed, also called river beauty, grows in the High Arctic.

No one knows for sure why the male NARWHAL has one long horn. (It's actually an overgrown tooth.) Could it help carry the narwhal's sound? Could it be a fencing sword? Or an ice-poker?

Large and powerful, the GLAUCOUS-WINGED GULL has a hooked yellow beak and pink feet. It can stand on the ice for hours at a time.

The ORANGE-GOLDEN BUMBLEBEE knows just where to get warm: in a bowl-shaped poppy. When the sunlight bounces off the petals, it pools in the center of the flower and warms the bee. The bumblebee also is able to warm itself by exercising its wings before flying.

The KILLER WHALE is really a large dolphin. They hunt in groups called pods. *Orca* is another name for killer whale.

 No animal on Earth moves faster than the PEREGRINE FALCON. Its dive from high in the sky has been timed at more than two hundred miles per hour.

 No bigger than a sparrow, the SNOW BUNTING is also known as the snowflake. It builds its nest in the Arctic during the summer. For winter, it migrates southward. Its reappearance signals the return of spring to the Arctic.

 Of all bears, the POLAR BEAR is the best swimmer. It can stay in icy Arctic waters for hours. It is all white except for its black nose. When sneaking up on a seal that is basking on the ice, the polar bear might put its nose down close to the rough ice surface so that the black color isn't noticeable.

 In autumn, the SNOW FLEA burrows into the ground. It produces a chemical that protects it from freezing—and so it survives the long Arctic winter.

 PTARMIGAN have a cuff of feathers around their feet. Ptarmigan walk more often than fly. When you say its name, don't pronounce the *P*.

 The soft downy feathers and the rounded wings of the SNOWY OWL enable this bird to fly almost silently across the tundra. Adult owls are usually pure white.

 RINGED SEALS are the smallest of all seals. There are more of them than any other kind of seal in the Arctic. Adults have dark spots surrounded by light-colored rings.

 The WALRUS is the only animal whose teeth help it walk. Using its tusks (which are overgrown teeth), it pulls itself out of the water and onto the ice. A walrus is actually a large type of seal.